"The Truth Shall Set You Free"

"The Truth Shall Set You Free"

Biblical truths that reveal God's plan for
financial freedom

Fred H. Waller

Foreword by
Louis A. Butcher, Jr.

Hosea 4:6 –
Not if I can help it!

Fred Waller
John 8:32

iUniverse, Inc.
New York Lincoln Shanghai

"The Truth Shall Set You Free"
Biblical truths that reveal God's plan for financial freedom

iUniverse books may be ordered through booksellers or by contacting:

iUniverse
2021 Pine Lake Road, Suite 100
Lincoln, NE 68512
www.iuniverse.com
1-800-Authors (1-800-288-4677)

ISBN-13: 978-0-595-40696-8 (pbk)
ISBN-13: 978-0-595-85060-0 (ebk)
ISBN-10: 0-595-40696-3 (pbk)
ISBN-10: 0-595-85060-X (ebk)

Printed in the United States of America

To my parents
Pastor Jacob C. Waller and Barbara Ann Waller

Thank you for modeling a loving, and caring spirit throughout your lives. I have excellent role models. Whatever people see in me, they would have to multiply that by thousands to see what is in both of you!

Contents

Foreword

One thing is for certain: Fred Waller has a passion for trying to persuade people to handle their finances God's way. His passion is driven by the instruction that God gives in His Word and the great benefits it brings to those who receive it and live by it. I have found that when I talk to Fred for more than a few minutes, the conversation will invariably turn to money and how it should be dealt with. But understand: the discussions are never overbearing or "preachy." More than likely, I am the one that will bring up the subject. I do so pleasantly, because I know I will learn something new as we talk.

Teaching seems to come naturally for this gifted young man. Having been a math teacher for a number of years, it is not difficult to sense immediately his ease of style and his ample ability to communicate. He is inspirational and brings an excitement to a subject that, quite frankly, can be boring.

Fred is well qualified to bring forth this competently written offering of fiscal information. He is a certified budget coach through Crown Financial Ministries and has worked as a mortgage specialist, assisting people in realizing the American dream of homeownership. He has encouraged his wife, Lynette, and others to become certified financial coaches as well.

What fascinates me about this book is his broad and effective use of Scripture to present and substantiate his positions. One gets the sense readily that this is not Fred, himself, speaking; rather it is the Holy Spirit revealing truth to him and his willingness to pass it on to us. Refreshingly, it became clear to me as I read that anyone, no matter how dire and desperate their financial situation, could benefit from this book and be encouraged to improve their condition. The outcomes work because they are prescribed by God.

In a society that values instant gratification and get-rich-quick schemes, where a person's worth seems to be measured by how many credit cards they have or how many possessions they have accumulated, it is uplifting to be reminded by Fred that the earth is the Lord's and nothing we possess really belongs to us.

Fred is a good father and definitely a family man. He and his wife have already begun teaching their two darling young daughters the value of money and assets and how to use them God's way. I only wish other parents would be as diligent as they raise their children. Following frivolous fads and trends can be very expensive, but that is exactly what many of our young people are doing today.

We are blessed at Bright Side Church to have a person of Fred's character in our presence. Not only does he serve as a deacon, he also heads up our Education Ministry Center. He teaches courses on finances and has networked with some of the premier Biblical financial advisors in the country.

I am already convinced that this is just the first in a long series of books that will bless readers with information on how God wants us to handle things. If this, his inaugural work, is any indication, we are in for a continuing treat.

All I can say is, "Be blessed, my Brother. Go Fred, go!"

Lancaster, Pennsylvania   Louis A. Butcher, Jr.
June, 2006   Pastor, Bright Side Baptist Church

Acknowledgements

To my wife Lynette: words cannot express the love I have for you and who you are. We are a living testimony to God's Word when He says that "all things work together for good for them that love the Lord and are called according to His purpose." All the things that we have gone through have been for the good of our marriage and our family. Let's continue to let our light shine. I love you!

To my beautiful daughters, Cheyanne and Kylee: you guys are so easy to love. Daddy will always work really hard to make sure you feel loved deep down on the inside.

To Juanita Waller: God has truly used you as a vessel for my spiritual growth. You have also inspired me more than you will ever know. Thank you!

To Ricky, Yolanda, Sunee', and Stephon: I love you guys very much!

To Pastor Louis A. Butcher Jr.: your teaching has truly allowed me to grow spiritually, and your great vision has inspired me to see things in a big way as well. Thanks for writing the foreword.

To Andrew Morrison: thank you for planting the seed for this book. Without our relationship, this book may not have become a reality. For that, I am thankful. Your business coaching continues to be a blessing to me.

To Lee Jenkins: you are a mighty general in this spiritual war against financial bondage. I am reporting for duty. I desire to do my part to win this war against financial bondage. I look forward to the continued growth of our friendship.

To Jason Wright: I always tell you that if I can be half as much a friend to you as you have been to me, I will accomplish a great thing. I truly am grateful that I have you as a friend A-PHIIIIIII

To Lee Strawbridge: who would have thought that we would both be published authors? I will race you to the Oprah show ☺ A-PHIIIIIII

To my Bright Side Church family: I truly enjoy my opportunities to serve and to be served at the church. Let's continue to grow together.

Introduction

Is God Your Pilot or Co-Pilot?

We have all seen the very popular bumper sticker "God is my co-pilot." God would probably want to edit that phrase because a co-pilot follows the instructions of the pilot, and "God is my co-pilot" implies that God follows our instructions. We should not try to set our own direction. Instead, we should seek the direction of our God. According to Psalms 23, David says that *"The Lord is my shepherd…" (Psalm 23:1 NIV)*. That powerful statement lets us know the position God should have in our lives. He should be our shepherd. What do shepherds do? They set the direction. They lead their sheep. We must be like sheep in the eyes of God. We have to be willing to take on a sheep's mentality. Sheep, by nature, have no direction of their own. They tend to wander aimlessly into dangerous situations. In relation to our finances, we have all wandered into dangerous situations at some point in our lives!

We also find out later in Psalms 23 that God *"leads [us] beside quiet waters"* and that He *"guides [us] in paths of righteousness…"* Nowhere in that passage does David say that God sits next to us as we lead and guide ourselves. Have we made God the co-pilot of our finances? If recent statistics concerning declining personal savings rates and increasing consumer debt are any indication, the answer is yes! One could argue that in matters of money, God is not even on the plane. If God is not on the plane, can we be sure that our plane will land safely? Would you risk it? I certainly wouldn't! It is time for us to make God the pilot and not the co-pilot of our finances. We need to get back under the direction of our shepherd. We can get back under His direction by learning about the biblical principles that can set us free financially. The Bible assures us that *"…you will know the **truth**, and the **truth** will set you free."(John 8:32 NIV)*. There are many biblical truths concerning how we should manage our money. When we understand them and apply them to our life, we can be set free-financially free!

I hope to share some insights on God's Word concerning managing money in a way that both encourages and challenges you. These pages will provide information that begins the process of transformation in your approach to managing what God has blessed you with. Throughout this book, we will explore biblical truths that teach us God's perspective on the many aspects of money management. Although, we are well aware of God's instruction on 10% of our money, it is time for us to learn what God says about managing the other 90%. These biblical truths about money management are powerful and life-changing because they teach us the "how to" and the "how come" of managing money.

My many years as a tax professional, budget coach, and money manager have taught me about the technical aspects of money management. I am president of Waller Tax and Money Advisors, a tax and money advisory firm that provides both tax return and money management services to hundreds of clients. I am also a Deacon at Bright Side Baptist Church in Central Pennsylvania. I am also the Chairman of the Education Ministry at my church. As Chair, my responsibilities include the developing, implementing and monitoring of the Christian Educational programs offered to our members and community. I have also spent many years in education as a math teacher. I am married to Lynette Waller, and we have two beautiful little girls, Cheyanne and Kylee.

As Deacon and Education Ministry chair at my church, I have many opportunities to serve and teach our congregation. God has used these opportunities to reveal some situations that are cause for concern. The enemy has used money to put Christians in financial bondage. The financial afflictions of the world have definitely found their way into the lives of Christians. Christians are dealing with bankruptcy, overwhelming debt, and grossly inadequate savings. It is not surprising that Christians have to battle against financial bondage. Satan knows that if we are financially bound, our ability to serve God is hindered. God tells us to go out and teach others about Him. He also wants us to work to advance His kingdom through our time, talents, and tithes. Unfortunately, financial bondage robs us of our time because we are forced to work longer hours to pay our debts. Our talents are often underutilized because of the time restraints put on us by our working. Tithing is something that we know we must do, but just don't have enough faith that God can provide our needs if we tithe. It is time to serve an eviction notice on these financial strongholds in our lives. They are no longer welcome in the household of faith. This book, with God's help, can help to break the financial strongholds in your life. We will use biblical truths to lift up a standard against these financial strongholds so that breakthroughs will occur.

I want you to imagine with me a three foot fence. On one side is God's way of managing money. On the other side is the world's way of managing money. Do you *"straddle the fence"* when it comes to making decisions? If we desire a better way to manage our money, we must firmly decide that God's way is the only way. This piece of work is firmly planted on the side of God's will. I believe that this is where true financial breakthroughs occur. That belief comes from firsthand experience of what God can do when you follow His money management plan. I am a living witness of what God can do when you follow His plan. God has tremendously blessed the 90% that he has entrusted me to manage. I know that I am experiencing a much better life on the 90% plan than I ever was on the 100% plan.

In 2 Corinthians 5:17(NIV), we are taught that *"Therefore, if anyone is in Christ, he is a new creation; the old has gone, the new has come!"* We can become new creatures when it comes to our finances if we are willing to let God in our finances. We should let go of our finances and let God have a chance to control them. Once we learn the biblical truths, we cannot argue with them. That is why a money management book from a biblical point of view should have more power to change our ways. That is why this book is firmly planted in God's way.

According to the July 10, 2006 Federal Reserve Consumer Credit data[1], Americans are in debt to the tune of over 2 trillion dollars. Yes-I said trillion with a T. The amount of debt that Americans are taking on is growing at a pace never before seen in American history. That debt load is being carried on the backs of many Christians. What happens when you carry too much on your back? Your back begins to hurt. When your back hurts, everything you physically do will be negatively impacted. When your finances are hurting, everything you do will be negatively impacted as well. Some of your life choices will be limited. I need to work out, but I cannot afford the gym membership. I would love to put my kids in private school, but I cannot afford the tuition. I know I need to tithe, but I cannot seem to be able to afford to do it. Most of the things that we should be doing have a price tag on them. If our finances are in turmoil, we will not be able to pay the price unless we use credit cards. That is why our debt situation is so bad.

I feel strongly that a lot of us suffer needlessly when it comes to our finances. In Hosea 4:6, we are told that *"...my people are destroyed from lack of knowledge." (Hosea 4:6 NIV)* What knowledge do we lack? Do we know what God says about credit? Do we know what God says about debt? Do we know what God says about saving and investing? Do we know what God says about getting advice? Until we understand the biblical truths that cover all of those things, we are at risk for destruction.

In this book, we will identify some biblical truths, or "bricks", that God desires us to use to build a strong financial house. Without these bricks, the financial houses we build will not be able to withstand financial storms. They may be able to stand for a while, but not withstand over a long period of time. Each one of the following bricks are vital to the strength of the entire financial house. If one of these "biblical bricks" is missing, the financial integrity of the house is compromised. One of God's "biblical bricks" deals with the foundation of our financial house. Our foundation should be cemented with the Word of God. The remaining bricks then deal with Credit, Debt, Giving, Saving/ Investing. Finally, the roof of proper estate planning is where the final bricks go. Over the next few pages, we will expose the "biblical bricks" that have to exist in order to build a strong financial house.

Before we get started, I feel led to say a word of prayer over this time that you will be reading this book. It is my prayer that God will honor this step you are taking to learn about His biblical truths concerning managing money. Bow your heads with me as I share a prayer:

*"Father God, I pray **right now** that this book, inspired by you, born out of experiences that you have guided me into and through, will serve as a tool that you anoint to break the strongholds of financial bondage that afflict*

many of the people in this world that we live in. You said in Your word that the effectual fervent prayer of the righteous availeth much, and so I fervently and faithfully pray that whomever You lead to this piece of work will be set free from financial bondage. May You be glorified through the testimony that they will share about how your biblical truths set them free from their financial bondage. In Jesus' name, I pray. AMEN!

Let us begin! I know you remember the story of the three little pigs. The mother sends her three sons off to live on their own with a warning to look out for the wolf. The three little pigs need a place to live, so they decide to build their own houses. The first pig builds his house out of straw. The second pig builds his house out of sticks. Building a house out of straw and sticks probably didn't take much effort. What do you think motivated the younger pigs to use straw and sticks? Well, you can build a home quickly with those materials. It also does not take much labor. Now, the third pig took his time to build his house. He decided to build his house out of bricks. You know the rest of the story. Unfortunately, the big, bad wolf huffed and puffed and blew down the house of the first and second pig. The wolf comes to the third house and proceeds to huff and puff, and huff and puff, and huff and puff, but to no avail. He could not blow down the house made of brick. Well, what about your financial house? Is your financial house built with straw, sticks, or is it built with bricks?" Better yet, is it built with "biblical bricks?"

When the "big bad wolf" of unexpected repairs, higher then expected bills, and all the other financial issues of today blows against your house, will it stand? The best way to insure that the answer will be yes is to build your house using God's bricks of biblical truths. With those bricks, you can insure a strong financial house.

1

Building a Foundation

"Except the LORD build the house,
they labour in vain that build it..."
(Psalms 127:1 KJV)

That first brick is so important in a strong financial house. Its importance is punctuated by the fact that it has four pieces. This brick goes into the foundation of a strong financial house. Without it, the other parts of the house, no matter how well they may be constructed, will fall down. The first brick deals with the following biblical truths:

- Truth #1: We must hear and obey God's word

- Truth #2: We must realize that our resources are not really "ours"

- Truth #3: We must understand our role and God's role

- Truth #4: We must seek and listen to advice

Truth #1 deals with hearing and obeying God's Word. I remember when I played video games as a child. There was a specific space game that I played all the time. Many of my days as a teenager were spent trying to master this game. The game was all I wanted to do. When my Mom needed me to either come eat, or do her a quick favor, she would call me. I would hear her, but because I was doing something that I felt was much more fun than what she wanted me to do, I would not obey her. "Fred!" she would yell once. I would hear her, but I wouldn't obey her. *"FRED!"* she would yell a little louder the second time. Once again, I definitely heard her, but I chose not to obey her. Then, the call that lets you know she wants you now and is tired of calling you. You know: the dreaded "full name call!" *"FREDERICK HENRY WALLER!"* That told me that she was tired of my disobedience and that I might want to obey her right now!

Fast forward twenty or so years, and not much has changed. This scenario of hearing and not obeying plays out just about every night in my house even to this day. As a matter of fact, it happened a few times as I was in the process of writing this book. When dinner is ready, Lynette calls me to eat. Well, I hear her, but I am normally doing some work on the computer that I think is more important then getting to dinner on time. So, I hear her, but I don't obey. She normally calls me about two more times before she just says *"The food is on the table, and I am eating!"*

These situations illustrate our own behavior when we deal with God as He speaks to us through His Word. We hear Him calling us, but we decide not to obey. This first biblical truth is vital to having a strong financial house. Matthew 7:24-27 shows us the importance and blessings that come from hearing and obeying. Our financial house is impacted either positively or negatively depending on our use of the "brick" of obedience.

"Therefore whosoever heareth these sayings of mine, and doeth them, I will liken him unto a wise man, which built his house upon a rock. And the rain descended, and the floods came, and the winds blew, and beat upon that house; and it fell not: for it was founded upon a rock. And every one that heareth these sayings of mine, and doeth them not, shall be likened unto a foolish man, which built his house upon the sand. And the rain descended, and the floods came, and the winds blew, and beat upon that house; and it fell: and great was the fall of it." (Matthew 7:24-27 KJV)

The scripture says:

"Therefore, whosoever heareth these sayings of mine, and doeth them, I will liken him unto a wise man, which built his house upon a rock."

The first part clearly identifies the conditions by which God's biblical truths operate. Do we see what the key to a strong financial house is? The key is that we must hear AND obey God's Word. Those two things together—hearing AND obedience—are necessary to unlock the promises in this passage. We hear the instructions God has for us concerning our finances but, do we obey them? Obedience has to be demonstrated through a specific action. I can scream to my wife *"I'll be there in a second!";* however, that does not substitute actually getting up and going to the dinner table. Have you ever told God, *"I'll be there in a second?"* We tell Him that when we hear about tithing and do not tithe. We also tell Him that when He calls for our time, and we do not obey. We also tell Him that when He tells us to use our gifts, and we procrastinate. Later parts of this book will go into more detail as to how we can specifically obey God's Word when it comes to managing money.

This biblical truth promises protection against things that would come against the financial house when hearing and obedience take place. The passage says

"And the rain descended, and the floods came, and the winds blew, and beat upon that house; and it fell not..."

Although the wise man's house was battered with rain, floods, and winds, the house was able to stand. It is powerful to point out that by being obedient to God's Word, you still will have to go through some financial storms. These storms serve to test the foundation. Just like a strong wind will test the construction of a roof, financial storms test the construction of your financial house. A wise man's financial house will stand up to the financial rains, floods, and winds because the wise man heard and obeyed God's Word in areas of managing money. By hearing and obeying, the house will not fall.

This truth also has a promise of consequences for the foolish man who heard but did not obey. If we do not fully understand God's Word, we run the risk of experiencing consequences of disobedience without even knowing that there are consequences.

*"And every one that heareth these sayings of mine, and **doeth them not**, shall be likened unto a foolish man, which built his house upon the sand."*

The Word of God is clear on the fact that just hearing the Word is not enough. This point cannot be stressed enough. We must hear and obey. The foolish man heard the Word but did not obey it. Have you heard God speak to you about aspects of your money and you did not obey? We have to actually take some steps towards obeying what the Word of God challenges us to do. We have to settle in our minds that we are willing to OBEY God's Word. When we hear but do not obey, the scripture makes clear the consequence:

"...the rain descended, and the floods came, and the winds blew, and beat upon that house; and it fell: and great was the fall of it."

It is interesting to note that the structure of the passage is consistent. Both the wise man and the foolish man had to deal with the fact that the rain descended, the floods came, and the winds blew. They are both subject to the same testing of their obedience. The only difference is the consequence. When we are wise, our financial house will not fall. When we do what the foolish man does, the result will be different. The scripture tells us:

"And great was the fall of it!"

A strong financial foundation must begin with the decision to hear and obey the Word of God. By reading this book, you are beginning the journey of hearing what the Word of God has to teach you about managing money. As believer's who desire to do the will of God, we must now put ourselves in position to hear God's Word and then obey His Word as it relates to managing money. By hearing and obeying, we are wise. By hearing and not obeying, we are a fool. God has some things He wants us to hear and obey concerning managing money. When we hear and obey, God promises that our house won't fall. We have two choices. Will we be wise or foolish? There is a promise in God's word for the wise man that hears and obeys. There is a consequence for the fool that hears but does not obey. Would you rather have the promise or the consequence? WISE choice!

Truth #2 deals with establishing ownership. Is it God or us who can really say that this is "MINE?"

My 3 year old is going through this phase that all kids go through. The *"MINE"* stage. My wife and I cringe when we hear our 3 year old say *"MINE."* There are a few reasons for this. For one, it worries us. It makes us feel that she is selfish. We wonder if she will be selfish as she grows up. It also is a little embarrassing when she is playing with our friends' kids and she snatches and says *"MINE."* Probably the most disturbing aspect of Kylee's saying this is the fact that it is not HERS! She does not own the toys that she is playing with. We bought those toys with our money. When we bought the toys, we intended for her to enjoy them and when the situation came up, she would share them. Now, instead of sharing, she is taking control of something that she does not have the right to control. As owners of the toy, we never transferred ownership to her. We maintain ownership but just allow her to use it. Have we become like self-absorbed kids when it comes to the money that God has blessed us with? We have to remember that God owns everything. He did not transfer ownership to us. The house we live in, the car we drive, and the bank account we withdraw from belongs to God. There is a biblical truth that illustrates this fact. In 1 Chronicles, we are taught about God's ownership when David prays to God after he and the Israelites contributed money and service to build the temple where the Ark of the Covenant would rest. This is the temple that David's son Solomon would eventually build. In 1 Chronicles 29, we are taught that:

"Wherefore David blessed the LORD before all the congregation: and David said, Blessed be thou, LORD God of Israel our father, for ever and ever. Thine, O LORD is the greatness, and the power, and the glory, and the victory, and the majesty: for all that is in the heaven and in the earth is thine; thine is the kingdom, O LORD, and thou art exalted as head above all. Both riches and honour come of thee, and thou reignest over all; and in thine hand is power and might; and in thine hand it is to make great, and to give strength unto all." (1 Chronicles 29:10-12 KJV)

The scripture starts off with *"Wherefore David blessed the Lord before all the congregation..."* David openly praised God for how He provided for him. We must be willing to boldly acknowledge God as our provider of everything. The scripture goes on to say *"...for all that is in the heaven and in the earth is thine..."* He goes on to say in verse 12 that *"Both riches and honour come of thee..."*

David exposes the biblical truth that must go into the foundation of a strong financial house. We have to settle in our minds that we do not own anything. It is not our stuff. We must begin substituting "HIS" when we want to say "MINE." God owns it, we do not. He has never transferred ownership of anything to us. He also reminds us in His Word that the cattle on a thousand hills belong to Him[1]. The silver and the gold are His as well[2]. We must have a shift in thinking from "what is mine is mine" to "what I thought was mine is actually HIS." All this stuff that we possess belongs to GOD. Once we acknowledge that this is not "MINE," we will then have the right perspective about money. We are not the owners. We are given the opportunity to use it. That opportunity comes with some expectations. God expects us to thank Him for the opportunity to use it and also to remember that it all belongs to Him. He also has established some procedures He will judge us on as it relates to how we handle the money He blesses us with.

Truth #3 teaches us about our role along with God's role in managing money. My wife and I have purchased a wonderful piece of technology that allows us to record and then watch our favorite shows when it is convenient for us. It is basically a digital recorder that allows us to record any television show we wish. There are two parts to it. The first part is the piece of equipment called a Digital Video Recorder (DVR). This DVR has an internal storage device that stores the TV shows we record. The second part is a service that organizes the TV shows in such a way that makes recording of the shows simple. With the push of a button, you can record a show you want to watch that is coming on later that day, week, or even that month. We use this service to record and keep up with a show called "The Apprentice" starring Donald Trump. The show follows a group of people competing for a chance to be hired by Donald Trump. The winner will become the apprentice responsible for overseeing a project for Trump. The competition revolves around the two groups competing on certain tasks. Some of those tasks involve marketing, advertising development, and/or product promotion. One group wins and the other group loses. The losing group goes before Donald Trump where he judges them. During this process, one of the members of the losing group is deemed to be the most ineffective group member. That person then hears the words that you work so hard not to hear, *"You're fired!"* The goal for each group member is to not be fired.

As I think about this show, another biblical truth comes to mind. There is a parable in the Bible that deals with someone being fired. In Luke, we find Jesus talking with his disciples. As He often did, He was teaching through a parable. The parable illustrates that God evaluates our performance when it comes to managing money. If we do not handle it the way He would have us to handle it, we can be fired.

Luke 16:1, 2 and 11 reveal powerful biblical principles that we must make part of the foundational brick if we desire a strong financial house. Luke 16:1-2 states:

"Jesus told his disciples: "There was a rich man whose manager was accused of wasting his possessions. So he called him in and asked him, 'What is this I hear about you? Give an account of your management, because you cannot be manager any longer." (Luke 16:1-2 NIV)

In this account, we find a rich man and his financial manager. This rich man had a manager to manage his wealth. The manager did not own the money. The manager was given the responsibility to take care of it in a responsible way. This can be interpreted as God giving us the responsibility to manage His "cattle on a thousand hills." God is the rich man and we are the managers of His belongings. We find out that the manager was accused of wasting the master's possessions. As we continue to read, we find out that the manager is called in and asked to explain himself. What would you say if God called you into His "office" and asked you to explain your management of His possessions? Would this be an appointment you would look forward to, or could you be informed that you have mismanaged His belongings, and are fired? Watch what the master asked him. *"What is this I hear about you…?"* We must be careful not to read the Bible too fast. When we do that, we might miss an important point. Don't miss the fact that the rich man said, *"What is this I <u>HEAR</u> about you…?"* It is interesting to note that the manager's handling of the master's possessions got so bad that it became known to the master from outside sources. The manager did not even have to say anything. The rich man was hearing negative reports from other sources. We must not let our financial situation get to the point where people will hear about it from other sources.

Because of the manager's poor handling of the rich man's resources, he was relieved of his duties.

"Give an account of your management, because you cannot be manager any longer."

In essence, the manager was fired! How about you? If this was the last month of your 3 month evaluation, would God allow you to retain your position as manager of His possessions or would He say, "you are fired?" In order to keep our positions, we must build strong financial houses knowing that God does evaluate our performance.

We will conclude our first brick of a strong financial house with verse 11 of Luke chapter 16.

"So if you have not been trustworthy in handling worldly wealth, who will trust you with true riches?" (Luke 16:11 NIV)

Jesus urges us to understand that the handling of money is a test to show our ability to handle the true riches. He will not trust us with financial, physical, or spiritual prosperity if we have not shown our ability to manage the finances we have been made steward over. Settle the matter once and for all that you will manage your finances with God as your supervisor. You have to report to Him frequently, and you do not want to be fired!

Truth #4 deals with God's desire that we seek advice when it comes to managing His money. God does not desire us to be independent people, but, interdependent people. We must be willing to seek counsel from three sources. Those sources are prayer, the Bible, and Godly counselors.

Whenever I get an opportunity, I like to share this story. I use this story to illustrate this biblical truth. Stop reading for a second and look at your left index finger. Are you doing it? Great! Now, imagine if a rash began to form on that finger. This rash concerned you, but you did not want to go to the doctor because you were afraid that you might be treated with an injection of some kind. You say to yourself that the rash is not as bad as the potential for receiving a needle. Basically, you rationalized that the rash was bad, but the perceived consequence was worse. You go a little longer, and now the rash has spread to your arm. At this point, you are fearful that it is a bigger deal then you originally thought. You make an appointment and go visit your doctor. The doctor examines your arm and says, *"How long have you had this!?!"* *"Oh, about 3 months,"* you reply. The doctor looks at you in amazement and then gives you the bad news. *"This rash has infected your arm. I have to amputate your arm!"* You sit back in your chair stunned. He then goes on to explain that normally this rash starts off as a harmless skin irritation. At that early stage, it can be easily treated with just a simple ointment. Unfortunately, when it spreads to the arm, it becomes much worse and can only be remedied with amputation. Now, in all fairness, I am not aware of a type of rash like this. I am just using this story to help illustrate a biblical truth found in Proverbs 12:15. The scripture states:

"The way of a fool is right in his own eyes: but he that hearkeneth unto counsel is wise" (Proverbs 12:15 KJV)

This Proverb is attributed to the one whom God blessed to be the wisest man on Earth[3]. That man was King Solomon. As we study this passage, we will see why a strong financial house must be built on a foundation that insists on seeking and obeying advice.

"The way of a fool is right in his own eyes:"

A fool only looks at things through his own eyes. A fool does not think that he is wrong. This is an extremely dangerous mindset to have. The financial decisions that are made from that foolish perspective oftentimes prove to be some of the worst financial decisions of our lives. When we think our plans are right, we do not feel the need to question those plans. I have a question for you. Does the direction you are taking in areas of your finances seem right through your eyes? If so, what about someone else's eyes? Have you ever given someone else a chance to examine your plans as it relates to the management of your money? We are taught in Proverbs that we should let other people examine our plans. Of course, we are not to let just anybody examine our plans. God's Word gives us clear instructions on how we are to seek counsel. In Ecclesiastes 4:9-12, we are encouraged to rely on others. The end of this passage tells us that *"…a threefold cord is not quickly broken."(Ecclesiastes 4:12 KJV)*. That threefold cord is prayer, the studying of the Bible, and seeking counsel from parents and godly counselors. Make sure you make every financial decision a spiritual decision that is prayed over, studied, and shared with a godly counselor.

Proverbs 12:15 ends with a wonderful definition for a wise man. You can be wise in areas of finance only when you *"hearkeneth unto counsel."*

I looked up what it meant to hearken in a bible dictionary and it said "to hear in order to obey or comply.[4]" There's that word obedience again. Must be important! This brings us back to the previous scripture in "Matthew" that dealt with hearing and obeying God. The Word of God calls on us to hearken to counsel. In areas of our finance, we must follow God's plan on seeking counsel. A requirement for a strong financial house is that the members of the house be willing to rely not just on their own eyes when it comes to decision making. Households must be willing to hearken to counsel. That counsel is provided by the threefold cord of prayer, study, and godly counselors. What we find when we seek counsel is that eventually God will not have to speak to us at every situation. It will be a part of our hearts which the Holy Spirit takes over. He will instruct us not to buy this, or make sure you save that.

We spent a significant amount of time on the first brick because it is so important. A strong structure is determined by how strong the foundation is. Our financial house has to be built on those four biblical truths. We must remember that hearing and obedience are vital to the strength of our financial foundation. God promises that when we hear and obey, our financial house will be able to withstand the financial storms that occur in our lives. We must also acknowledge the biblical truth concerning ownership. We must remember that there is no such thing as MINE when it comes to money. We do not own anything. It all comes from God. When we have truly allowed the "Mine" mentality to die, the "His" mentality can live. At that point, we are being the faithful stewards that God desires us to be. We must also remember that we are held accountable for managing God's possessions. If we are not faithful, we can be fired. Finally, we must not have an independent spirit when it comes to dealing with money. We must seek, listen to, and obey wise counsel. That wise counsel comes through prayer, studying of the Bible, and through godly counselors.

2

Protecting Your Good Name

"A good name is more desirable than great riches;
to be esteemed is better than silver or gold." (Proverbs 22:1 NIV)

As a mortgage broker, my job was to examine the credit reports and other financial information of potential borrowers. I would use that information to determine whether they qualified for a loan. Too often, the credit reports that I would examine had credit scores that made it difficult to qualify for a loan. Divorce, health issues, or lost income represented a small percentage of the reasons for the low credit scores. Those reasons typically are not things that we can control. Unfortunately, the majority of the credit reports had low scores because of something that we can control. I saw a large percentage of low credit scores because of late payments. There would be bills on the credit report that were 30 days, 60 days, and sometimes even 90 days late. When bills are frequently paid late, it is very difficult to qualify for a loan. When people find out that they cannot qualify for a loan to purchase a home, they become disappointed and discouraged. I often found myself wishing that someone had shared with them the importance of proper credit management. A strong financial house must make proper credit management a priority.

When I teach at my workshops, I always tell the audience that I hide behind the Word of God. I try to use scriptures to support any thoughts that I have concerning the managing of money. There are biblical truths that teach us about the importance of proper credit management. Proverbs 3:27-28 teaches us to

"Withhold not good from them to whom it is due, when it is in the power of thine hand to do it. Say not unto thy neighbour, Go, and come again, and tomorrow I will give; when thou hast it by thee." (Proverbs 3:27-28 KJV)

We are first taught to not keep money from anybody we owe when we have the ability to pay. We must pay our bills and pay them when they are due. Well, some would say *"I would love to pay the bills when they are due, but, I have so many bills and not enough money."* I have heard it said that we can sometimes suffer from "too much month and not enough money." We must take that a step further and uncover how we got in that situation to begin with. Did we purchase things on credit that we did not need? Did we not seek counsel when it came to purchasing that big ticket item like a car or motorcycle? Some of us have obligated ourselves to monthly payments for things we do not even need. All of those payments have made it difficult to keep up. Do you feel that way? If you do, ask God to examine whether or not you have made financial decisions that have put you in a tough situation. Then, pray that He forgives you and pilots you out of those tough situations.

The scripture then instructs us not to say to our neighbor, *"come at another time even when you know you have it now."* We are not guaranteed the tomorrow that we promise someone. *"Tomorrow I will give"* makes the assumption that God has promised us the years it would take to pay those monthly bills. If God has blessed us with the resources to take care of our responsibilities, then He expects us to do that when it is due.

Proverbs 22:1 gives us more scriptural foundation for being a strong financial house using the brick of proper credit management.

"A good name is more desirable than great riches; to be esteemed is better than silver or gold."(Proverbs 22:1 NIV)

This biblical truth lets us know that we should desire a good name more than we desire wealth. Do you ever get the feeling that this world has reversed this scripture? The world seems to think that great riches are more desirable than a good name. I will get ahead by any means necessary. Not only should we desire a good name, we must do the things that allow us to earn a good name. This is especially vital in the area of proper credit management. Here are some specific steps to take to insure a good name through your credit report.

Step 1: Get a copy of your credit report.

Once a year, you can receive a free copy of your credit report. A great website for that is www.annualcreditreport.com. A great way to put the biblical truth of hearing and obedience in action would be to stop now and go to the website to request your free credit report. I went to the site and it took about 2 minutes to review my credit report. Once you get it, print it out and look through it carefully. If you happen to identify errors on the report, begin the process to change it. The best way to make adjustments to your credit report is to begin with the creditor that is reporting the mistake. Your credit report will have every single creditor and their contact information. Call the creditor to see if the mistake is a simple one that can be easily fixed. If they cannot or choose not, call the credit agency that is reporting the mistake and request a "dispute form." Send the completed "dispute form" back to the credit agency. By law, they must respond within 30-45 days. If you must contact them by letter, send the "dispute request" letter by certified mail. Your letter just needs to communicate who you are and that you are requesting a "dispute form." They require that you sign the letter and include your social security number. All of the credit bureau contact information should be on your credit report.

Step 2: Develop the habit of paying your bills on time through the "divide and conquer" strategy

We learn from credit reporting agencies that if you pay a bill 30 days late, your credit score could drop by as much as 20 points. On the other hand, consistently paying bills on time will increase your score by as much as 30 points. Lack of a system to pay your bills is typically the reason for late payments. Is that your problem? If so, consider having your bills automatically deducted from your bank account. That insures that the bill is paid on time.

My budget coaching experience has really taught me a lot about how people in tough financial situations pay their bills. I typically see that people are paying their bills based on when the bills come into the house. Some bills come around the 1st of the month. Some bills come in the middle, and some come at the end. I call that strategy the *"pay as it comes"* strategy. When the bill comes, they see what is in their account. If there is enough, they pay the bill. If there is not enough, they have to wait until the next check and pay it then. Unfortunately, while waiting for the next check, a few more bills come in that need to be paid. At that point, the paycheck you just received is not enough to cover the bills that have come in. That is when the cycle of late payments begins. This *"pay as it comes"* strategy is more of a reactive approach than a proactive one. I would like to propose a more proactive approach to paying bills.

We have all heard the cliché', *"divide and conquer."* We split something up so that it can be dealt with easily. The Bible tells us, and I paraphrase, that a house divided against itself cannot stand[1]. That biblical principle can be used in a positive way if we look at our bills as a house we want to divide. We can *"divide and conquer"* our bills. Lynette and I have managed our money using that principle and it has really simplified the paying of the bills. Instead of a reactive *"pay as it comes"* strategy, we have utilized the *"divide and conquer"* strategy. This strategy, if done consistently, can have a tremendous impact on the managing of your bill payments. The first thing you need to do is figure out how much money you consistently receive from whatever source of income you have. If you are a salaried employee, identify your net pay. If you are hourly and can count on a specific amount of consistent hours, use the net pay from that amount. If you are on 100% commission, it may be a little tougher but not impossible. I tell my clients in those situations to conservatively predict the amount of commission income you will receive per month. Use that figure as your net pay. I don't advise the including of overtime or bonuses in any of these figures. They are too infrequent to develop a workable budget. I believe that workable budgets deal with the core funds that are easily predicted.

The second step is to identify when you receive that income. Are you paid once a week, once every two weeks, or once a month? Your bills are then treated as being "paid" every week, once every two weeks, or once a month. Both your income and your bills are put on the same schedule. Most of our bills can be fairly predictable in their amount. Our mortgage or rent is a set amount each month. Our car payment and car insurance are set amounts each month. Most phone, utility and oil companies provide convenient budget billing which can make those bills predictable every month. Each predictable bill is split based on the frequency of the income. For example, the mortgage payment is split into four equal payments to reflect a once a week pay period. It would be split into two equal payments to match up with getting paid every two weeks. Or, it would be left as one payment if paid once a month.

An example should help to clarify this. I have included an example using our gas bill. First thing we did was call our gas company and request to have our bill converted to budget billing. Before budget billing, we would have a high gas bill in the winter and a low one in the summer. Now, our gas bill is $91.00 a month. In December, it is $91.00. In July, it is $91.00. Prior to budget billing, the December bill could have been as high as $200.00 and the July bill could've been as low as $25.00. That inconsistent bill made the paying of the bill very difficult to manage. With the budget program, we have a consistent $91.00 bill. I might want to mention that these budget programs that I talk about are available to everyone. These are not programs for low income households. They are specifically designed to assist those of us who manage our money using some form of a budget.

My household receives a paycheck every two weeks. Other than two times a year, we always get two paychecks in a month. That means our income comes in twice, therefore our bills must be divided into two. Let's say our first paycheck comes in on the 14th of July. From that paycheck, we set aside $45.50 to pay the gas bill. Even though we have not actually received the gas bill, we know it is coming. We set the money aside by writing in our check ledger $45.50 as a subtraction. When the bill comes in on the 16th to be paid by the 30th, we know that we have one more pay on the 28th. The pay on the 28th will be used to finish the $45.50 for a total of $91.00. The money will then be available when it is deducted automatically. That way, my gas bill is paid by both of my paychecks. We have basically divided the gas bill into the two paychecks that we know come in and therefore conquered the gas bill. We use this strategy with most of our bills.

The *"pay as it comes"* approach is not good management of money. That approach does not allow every paycheck to pay its share of every bill that comes in. Instead, identify all of your bills and make sure each paycheck that comes into the house is held responsible for paying its fair share of each bill.

Step 3: Decreasing your debt to credit ratio.

Proper credit management also involves the proper management of debt. The best way to manage debt is get rid of it. However, as you move towards that debt-free life by paying down credit card debt, you are helping to achieve that good name through achieving a strong credit score. The relationship between how much money you presently owe and how much money you have the capacity to owe is considered your debt to credit ratio. For example, if you have a $1,000 limit on your credit card and you owe $800.00 on that credit card, your debt to credit ratio is 80%. You owe 80% off what you have the ability to owe. That is extremely high. That basically sends the message that when you get credit, you use it all up. As much as creditors like to give you credit, credit agencies don't like to see you use a lot of it. Your credit score is lowered as that ratio percentage goes higher. On the flip side, if you have a $1,000 limit and owe $200.00, your debt to credit ratio is 20%. That ratio is low enough to possibly increase your credit score. The increase is due to the fact that credit agencies see that as proper credit management. You have $1,000 but are only using a small percentage of it. If you are encouraged that your credit score would go higher with a lower debt to credit ratio, just imagine what your credit score would be with a 0% debt to credit ratio. That would mean that I have a $1,000 credit card that I don't owe a balance on. Proper credit management includes decreasing your debt to credit ratio to 0%! After you have paid the credit card off, close the account and cut it in half!

The second brick lets us know the importance of the proper management of our good name. We must remember that we are encouraged to desire a good name more than riches. We do that by not withholding payment when we have the power to pay. We also need to pray that God will honor our obedience as we promptly pay our bills by helping to get rid of monthly obligations that make it difficult to pay bills on time. Once we have the biblical perspective on proper credit management, we can then work towards this from a practical perspective. We then should get a copy of our credit report. Pay our bills on time and decrease our debt. By doing those things, we are building a strong financial house using one of God's bricks.

3

Financial Bondage

*"The rich ruleth over the poor,
and the borrower is servant to the lender"
(Proverbs 22:7 KJV)*

The third brick in a strong financial house deals with biblical truths concerning debt. My pastor often times says *"When God says it, that settles it."* Well God's Word is clear in Romans 13:8 when He instructs us to

"Owe no man anything…" (Romans 13:8 KJV)

There are many scriptures in the bible that deal with the concept of servant. As I began to look at these passages, it became clear that most of the scriptures identified a servant as either a servant of a man or a servant of God. No matter how the word servant was used, it was describing a situation where either a man or God was the master. This is an interesting revelation when you lift up Proverbs 22:7 which states,

"The rich ruleth over the poor, and the borrower is servant to the lender." *(Proverbs 22:7 KJV)*

According to the dictionary, "servant" means *"One who yields obedience to another."*[1] When we are in debt, we yield our obedience to someone other than God. Instead of serving God, we have to serve the MASTER-card. We are reminded in scripture that we cannot serve two masters.[2] How does God want us to serve Him? We must serve Him by obeying His will for our lives. His will for us is our purpose in life. Well, how do we find out what our purpose in life is? One way we can get an idea of our purpose is to answer this question. *"If money where no object, what would you be doing with your time?"* When I ask that question in a workshop, smiles immediately fill the room. There are various responses to that question. When people answer that question, they are getting an idea of their purpose. People would say that "I would volunteer more!" I would give more to my church! I would quit my job and go work in another profession!" Unfortunately, the next question turns the smiles into frowns. *"Well, why aren't you living out those desires?"* Too many financial obligations make it difficult to live out those desires. Debt becomes the thief that robs us of our ability to live out our purpose. God desires us to live out the purpose that He has created us for. We are taught that *"[We] were bought at a price; do not become slaves of men."*(1 Corinthians 7:23 NIV) When Jesus shed His blood, He redeemed us so that we may have a relationship with His Father. That is a relationship of service. When our finances are in turmoil, it makes it difficult to obey His will for our life. That is why getting rid of debt is the third brick in a strong financial house.

Another biblical truth for building a strong financial house is illustrated in Psalms 37:21. We are taught that:

"The wicked borrow and do not repay, but the righteous give generously" *(Psalm 37:21 NIV)*

In this scripture, God is calling someone wicked if they borrow and do not repay. There are some interesting things that come out of this particular passage. One interpretation could be that if we borrow, and do not repay, we are considered wicked in the eyes of God. A not so obvious interpretation also comes out when we think about the fact that wicked people are put in position, unfortunately, to have to borrow. Their having to rely on debt probably stems from their disobedience to God's will with their finances. If you go back to Deuteronomy, God lays out to His children that disobedience to God and His commands will lead to a multitude of curses. One of the curses was that:

"The alien who lives among you will rise above you higher and higher, but you will sink lower and lower. He will lend to you, but you will not lend to him."(Deut 28: 43, 44 NIV)

The biblical truth is clear. God's financial plan instructs us to stay away from debt as much as we can. Freedom from debt eliminates one of the obstacles that keeps us from living out our purpose. If we can not live out our purpose, we can not serve God 100%.

Now that we are equipped with what God's perspective is on debt, let's look at some specific steps we can take to move from being a servant of debt to being a servant of the Most High.

First thing we must do to get out of debt is to pray. As we go through the debt reduction process, we must continue our prayers that God will find favor in us because of our steps of obedience. The Bible says that the fervent prayers of the righteous availeth much. This road out of debt will be a long, hard one. We may be wrapped up with years and years of debt bondage. It may take years and years to unwrap ourselves. We can, however rejoice in the fact that God can move supernaturally to strip away debt from our lives.

When I began my road out of financial bondage, I saw a sign that said "Debt Freedom, 1,000 miles" As I let God be my pilot, I would find myself driving down the road out of financial bondage and seeing a sign that said "Debt Freedom, 500 miles" and I had only driven 100 miles. I had numerous praise reports on how God showed up in miraculous ways to remove debt from my life. One in particular always stood out. I was home one day when I received an interesting phone call. I used to own a few rental properties. The handyman that I used when my rental properties needed work had called me. This was interesting because he normally didn't call me, I called him. However, on that night he called and inquired about whether or not I was interested in selling one of my rental properties. Now, I had been in prayer over selling one of my rentals. I actually had one on the market. Ironically, the one I had on the market, he was not interested in. He was, however, interested in one that I had planned on selling a year later. I did not want to sell that property because it needed a lot of exterior cosmetic work. The brick was crumbling away from the front exterior. This wasn't a dangerous situation but it would have a negative impact on its curb appeal when I tried to sell it. I believe that it was God's answer to my prayers that the handyman did not mind the brick work. Long story short, within about three weeks, I sold the property to him and was free from one of my largest financial burdens. That property had me financially bound, but God supernaturally released me from that bondage. I believe that God found favor in me for the steps I had been taking to get out of debt.

As you stay in prayer over your debt situation, you must also do a few more things. You need to:

1. List your debts

A journey of a thousand miles begins with a first step. After we pray, we need to identify our starting point. I encourage you to put this book down and grab a piece of paper. On that piece of paper, I want you to write down all of your debts. Seriously, you should do this right now. I realize that you may not have all of the important details, but get some basic information down. Awareness is a powerful motivator. By writing down all your debts, you become more keenly aware of your debts. That awareness will generate the reactions necessary to motivate you to continue through the debt reduction process. At a later point, you will complete this assignment by finding out some important details about your debt. The contact number, interest rate, and the total amount owed are important details to know about your debt. You can use the Debt list that I have included in the Appendix.

2. List some of God's "stuff"

It is at this moment that we are reminded of God's ownership of everything. He owns it, but has required that we be stewards of His "stuff." List some of your assets. Your assets include items such as your car, house, motorcycle, furniture, timeshare in Florida, etc. List all the things that are in your possession. I don't mean you take inventory of your socks, and underwear, but identify possible items that you could sell. With online auction companies being such a wonderful resource, you can have a virtual garage sale quickly. If you are not tech savvy, you can look for community yard sales to participate in.

It is at this time you may begin to hear God speak to you a word of conviction. Is God saying anything to you about your car payment? Is He speaking to you about the house that you bought that has payments that make it difficult to do anything else? That is called being "house-poor." Is that rental property that you have truly a blessing, or is it a stress in your life. Some of what we think are blessings in our lives actually are not. God says that *"The blessing of the LORD, it maketh rich, and he addeth no sorrow with it."(Proverbs 10:22 KJV)* If you are experiencing sorrow associated with any of these items, it is not a blessing from God. If it is not, you should look to do away with it. It's been said that it is hard to make a right decision, but harder to make a wrong decision right. After you have listed all of your assets, pray that God directs you as to what He wants you to do with them. Selling some of them can help you to get out of debt.

3. Create and Operate from a Budget

A wise man once said that "We do not know where our money went because we did not tell it where to go!" We tell our money where to go by developing the "B" word. At this point, you should have listed your debts, and identified assets that can be sold. You now need to deal with the "B" word. Yes, a budget. Your budget is your household's plan on how you are going to spend money. Some feel that a budget is restricting. Actually, a budget that properly reflects all your needs and wants can be a financially liberating experience. Our budget has a portion of money set aside for all of our needs and some of our wants. Some of the items can be considered both a need and a want. The clothing category is considered both a need and a want. If there is enough to purchase a nice suit, then I can purchase that suit guilt-free. I don't feel guilty because I know that this money is not for anything but clothing. We also have "eating out" as a budgeted item. When we go to our favorite restaurant, we know that we are spending cash specifically set aside for "eating out." These expenses do not affect whether or not we can pay our mortgage. Our mortgage has its own place in our budget.

What is the best way to create a realistic budget? My years as a budget coach have taught me strategies that have been successful in creating a realistic budget. Keep a 30 day diary of what you spend. This is crucial to developing a custom budget. Most people fail with their budget because they create a budget that is not customized for them. By tracking your spending, you become more aware of your spending habits. Did you buy coffee along with a newspaper on the way to work? If you did, write it down. Did you get gas today? If so, write it down. Did you spend $1.85 for a slice of lemon cake at your favorite coffee house-like my wife does? If so, write it down. Do this for 30 days and then review your spending. Many of my "coaching participants" have shared with me how eye opening this process is. When my wife and I did it, we could not believe how much money we were spending frivolously. Some of our wasteful spending added up to hundreds of dollars a month. After you have tracked your spending, you will begin to look at putting your spending plan down on paper or electronically. Your spending plan should address every foreseeable expense that your family has. Not only do you carve out money for the core expenses like the electric, phone, gas, mortgage, etc., you must also carve out money for non-routine expenses like occasional car repairs, holiday and birthday gifts, hair care, etc.

I have included an Excel spreadsheet on the companion CD for this book. It is a fully functional budget spreadsheet that my wife and I have found success with. You can use it as it is or customize it to meet your needs. The companion CD is available at my website, <u>www.</u> <u>FredWallerMinistries.com</u>.

4. Get out of debt

We are instructed to *"Owe no man anything…"* Once we identify whom we owe, we must then develop and diligently carry out a plan to pay off those debts. The Bible lets us know that *"The plans of the diligent lead to profit as surely as haste leads to poverty."*(Proverbs 21:5 NIV). Diligently working your debt elimination and spending plan will insure a profit. Your profit can manifest itself in a variety of ways such as getting your debts paid off more quickly, allowing your income to stretch further than you anticipated, or just having peace of mind when it comes to the management of money. Paying off debt is vital to the long term strength of your financial house. Just imagine what life would be like if your monthly expenses did not include those payments to creditors. What could you accomplish if you did not have those credit card bills or loan payments? When Lynette and I finally paid off all of our credit cards, we literally gave ourselves a $600 raise per month. That was how much we were spending in credit card bills per month! By paying off the debt, we were able to send our kids to private school. That would have never been possible if we were still in financial bondage to those MASTER-cards. So, what is the best way to get out of debt? There really isn't one best way to get out of debt. The best way will be the way for you that would yield you the greatest success. The road out of debt must have signs that let you know that you are getting close to your destination. When I travel a long distance, I am encouraged when I see a sign that lets me know my destination is 45 miles away. I get even more excited as I continue driving and see a sign that says that I am only 30 miles away. Any debt plan should have a component that allows you to experience results early and often. I want you to take a moment and imagine racing around the track against four other runners. As you start off, you quickly slip behind the other runners. You immediately begin to doubt your ability to win. Just as you begin to think through the ways you can bow out graciously, you begin to close in on the closest runner to you. You muster up just enough energy to pass him. As you pass him, you immediately begin to feel encouraged. That small success has just motivated you to go after the next runner closest to you. You are not even finished with the race, but you are motivated because of the success you experienced on the way.

A diet plan is another powerful parallel situation for the proper mindset necessary for any debt reduction plan to work. Imagine a diet plan. You are motivated to continue a diet plan when you step on the scale and see results throughout your program. Small successes keep you motivated to continue the journey. Don't concern yourself with how you are going to pay off your house. Focus your concern on how you are going to pay off your $116.00 store credit card bill. Once you pay that off, you get energized by that success. That feeling motivates you to want to experience that feeling again and this time on the $589.00 electronics store credit card bill. At that point, you can then look into some of the bigger debts. Your debt reduction plan must allow you to achieve short term success.

Well, what are some specific steps you can take to get out of debt? Some financial advisors recommend that you identify your highest debt and pay that off first. While that might make mathematical sense, it does not factor in the effect that paying off smaller debts has on our motivation. I recommend that you identify the smallest debt that you owe and develop, in your spending plan, a plan to pay that off quickly through extra payments. For example, say you owe $412.00 on a credit card and $3,256 on another credit card. The minimum payment on the $412.00 is just $20.00 and the minimum payment on the $3,256.00 is $80.00. That adds up to a minimum of $100.00 in monthly debt obligations. Your spending plan—which should be focused on debt reduction early on—says that you have $200.00 to allocate to debt reduction. I would pay the minimum on the $3,256.00 which would be $80.00 and the remaining $120.00 on the $412.00. Using simple math, and not accounting for interest, you would have the $412.00 paid off in less than five months. Once you have paid off that debt, you get motivated to pay off the next one. You then take that $120 and add it to the $80 for a total of $200.00. That $200 is then used to pay off the $3,256.00. Now continue to repeat that with all your debts until you are done.

5. Create additional income

I heard it said that the best place to go when you need money is......to work! A part time job is a wonderful step to take to pay down debt. This part time job is not your long term plan, but it is just a way of quickly inserting additional money into your budget for paying off debt. Now, let me encourage you to have a serious conversation with your family. God places a high priority on family and does not want your family negatively impacted by you working long hours. Let your family have input in the parameters that should be set as far as additional time and energy that you put forth. The decision to pick up more hours is only to help pay off your debts faster. Some financial experts say you can consider creating additional income through launching a business venture. I don't encourage that step. Actually, I would strongly discourage that. Now, as an entrepreneur myself, I am always pro-business. However, the infancy stage of a business is very time consuming and can also prove to be a costly endeavor. I don't recommend you try to launch a business during a time when you are overwhelmed with debt. Let your desire to start a business motivate you to work your debt reduction plan. When your debts are paid off, you will have those payments back in your control. You can then ask God if He desires that you launch a business. If it is in His will for you to do that, then, you can allocate those funds that were used for your debts to now fund your business venture.

6. Spend Cash as much as you can

An interesting study was done by a noted psychologist, Drazen Prelec. His main research and work focused on the psychological aspects of money. In one of his research studies, he set out to better understand what goes on psychologically when we spend money. He organized a silent auction and used his college students as bidders. He auctioned off a pair of tickets to a sold out NBA playoff game. The students were divided into two groups. Half of the bidders could only pay cash and the other group of bidders could only pay with a credit card. The results were stunning, even to the researchers. The researchers reported that on average, credit card buyers were willing to bid more than twice as much as the cash buyers.[3] They concluded that something happens psychologically that controls our spending to the point where we spend less when we spend cash. We don't experience the same reaction when we spend money with a credit card.

Most recently, the fast food restaurants have installed credit card machines. You can now use your credit card to purchase a "Number Three" with a large Coke. I always thought that the fast food industry was just responding to the popularity of the use of debit cards. However, I later found out that there were possibly some other reasons. According to a recent article from the National Council on Economic Education, certain fast food restaurants report that

"the cost of orders purchased using credit cards average 50% more than orders for which customers pay by checks or cash."[4]

We are probably going for the size increase and adding an apple pie just because we are using our credit card.

All of these reasons point to the fact that as many purchases as possible should be done with cash. The process of reaching in your pocket, pulling out $112.00 and pealing away $82.00 of it to purchase a pair of shoes, will definitely make you think twice about those shoes. Spend cash whenever you can.

7. Watch God move!

Money management from a Biblical point of view is necessary. When we want to do things our way, God's biblical principles show us why we should do it His way. These principles also provide us the direction on how to do it His way. These biblical principles also inspire us to press on through the difficult times. There is an extremely powerful biblical principle that gives us hope as we journey out of our financial bondage. II Kings 4:1-7 details one of the miracles done by God through Elisha. The scripture states:

"Now there cried a certain woman of the wives of the sons of the prophets unto Elisha, saying, Thy servant my husband is dead; and thou knowest that thy servant did fear the LORD: and the creditor is come to take unto him my two sons to be bondmen. And Elisha said unto her, What shall I do for thee? tell me, what hast thou in the house? And she said, Thine handmaid hath not any thing in the house, save a pot of oil. Then he said, Go, borrow thee vessels abroad of all thy neighbours, even empty vessels; borrow not a few. And when thou art come in, thou shalt shut the door upon thee and upon thy sons, and shalt pour out into all those vessels, and thou shalt set aside that which is full. So she went from him, and shut the door upon her and upon her sons, who brought the vessels to her; and she poured out. And it came to pass, when the vessels were full, that she said unto her son, Bring me yet a vessel. And he said unto her, There is not a vessel more. And the oil stayed. Then she came and told the man of God. And he said, Go, sell the oil, and pay thy debt, and live thou and thy children of the rest." (II Kings 4:1-7 KJV)

As we unpack this scripture, I want to highlight some interesting aspects that should both instruct us and encourage us. This passage instructs us on what we must do to invite God's presence as we grapple with our debts. We can also be encouraged by how God responded to the needs of this widow. The scripture begins with an introduction of the situation,

"Now there cried a certain woman of the wives of the sons of the prophets unto Elisha, saying, Thy servant my husband is dead; and thou knowest that thy servant did fear the LORD: and the creditor is come to take unto him my two sons to be bondmen..."

It is interesting to learn that the husband, who is not mentioned by name, happened to be a man of God. Fearing the Lord meant that you obeyed the will of God. In spite of that, he somehow got himself in a situation where he passed away with debt. This man has a place in scripture not because of his work as a man of God, but, because of his lack of provision for his family. His life work had been overshadowed by the fact that he left his wife and two sons in a position of potential servitude because of his debts.

The passage then continues with

"And Elisha said unto her, What shall I do for thee? tell me, what hast thou in the house? And she said, Thine handmaid hath not any thing in the house, save a pot of oil."

The man of God, after hearing the problem, questions the widow about what she has in her house. It is great to see that the man of God begins with having the woman look at what she has at her disposal. Do you sometimes think that God needs to bless you with more money, or a better job, or a better life, or that something has to happen to you for things to get better? God basically has made provision for you through what He has already blessed you with. You know that God would not put more on you than you can bear. However, that scripture does not say that YOU will not put more on YOU than you can bear. Elisha helps you to understand that more often than not, a financial break-through is well within YOUR reach. You just need a godly counselor to point out something that is right within your reach. That is why it is important to seek and then listen to wise counsel.

The response of the woman is indicative of a person overwhelmed with her situation. She says that all she has is this jar of oil. This little bit can't possibly help me, she seems to think. What you will see later in the scripture is that what she thought was a little bit in her eyes, was more than enough in the eyes of God.

The passage then continues with,

"Then he said, Go, borrow thee vessels abroad of all thy neighbours, even empty vessels; borrow not a few. And when thou art come in, thou shalt shut

the door upon thee and upon thy sons, and shalt pour out into all those vessels, and thou shalt set aside that which is full."

After she shares with Elisha that all she has is a small jar of oil, Elisha gives her instructions. Go get some empty jars, and make sure you get a lot. Using your spiritual imagination, just imagine the thoughts that could have gone on in the head of the woman. *"Well, if I go ask my neighbors, they are going to want to know why! I will be embarrassed. I also can't understand why I have to get a lot of empty jars."* As far as she could see, this was not moving her in the direction of taking care of the problem. She could not see the purpose for this. That is where our faith has to show up in a mighty way. According to Hebrews 11,

"Now faith is the substance of things hoped for, the evidence of things not seen." (Hebrews 11:1 KJV)

The Word of God says that your faith is the evidence of things not seen. That means that you won't see the evidence through your eyes. You will only see it through a faithful eye. Oftentimes we think that God has failed us, when in actuality it is our faith that has failed. Her obedience to the man of God to go in a direction that did not necessarily make sense to her was a faith test. Did she have enough faith to pass the test? This whole battle with finances is a faith test. Probably some of what has been shared so far in this book will test your faith. As you will see from this passage, God chose not to move until her faith was challenged and she passed the test. That is a very powerful principle to get down in your spirit. God typically shows up supernaturally only after we do a few things. We must first decide that we need His help. God is not pushy. He will not intervene unless He is asked to. After we ask for help, we must be willing to hear AND obey the advice. We hear from God when we seek Him. God moves when we have faith and obey what He says. The Bible lets us know that without faith, it is impossible to please God. If we don't please God, He will not find favor in our actions.

As we continue to unpack the scripture, you see the widow instructed to take her sons and close the doors. Pour the oil in the jars and put aside the jars that are full. As you can see from the remaining text, God shows up and honors her obedience, and rewards her faith by moving supernaturally.

And it came to pass, when the vessels were full, that she said unto her son, Bring me yet a vessel. And he said unto her, There is not a vessel more. And the oil stayed. Then she came and told the man of God. And he said, Go, sell the oil, and pay thy debt, and live thou and thy children off the rest."

The empty jars were filled through God's power to multiply the oil that the widow already had. When the empty jars were full, the oil stopped flowing. She then went to tell Elisha what had happened. That is a powerful principle as well. The man of God had instructed her on what she should do. He did not stay on her to make sure she did it. If he did that, he would have been impacting the woman's actions. She probably would have done it because she did not want to disappoint him. That is not faith. Elisha went somewhere and left the woman to make her decision to be obedient to God's will or not. She desired to obey God's will, and not to please Elisha.

When she went to tell Elisha about how God had moved, Elisha instructed the widow to take the oil that God had supernaturally increased and use it to do two things. There was enough provision to sell the oil and pay down the debt and then live off the rest. What is interesting here is that we don't know if the widow actually obeyed Elisha. She had just come out of a tough financial situation and now has more money than she ever thought possible. Now, I wonder if fear did not creep into her and make her make some alternative decisions. *"Maybe I will pay off some of my debts and put the rest aside for another emergency!"* Do you sometimes have to deal with the same fear? You come out of tough situations through God's supernatural intervention and then have to make a tough decision. Do you wonder if God can provide again? This sounds like another faith challenge. So, rejoice in how God can move when your faith is challenged and you walk by faith and not by sight.

As I close our conversation on what God desires our mindset to be on debt, I want to echo a few important points. First, we are not to be servants to anybody but God. We must get out of debt so we do not become a *"servant to the lender."* We must follow those steps I described diligently. We can take the story of the widow as both instruction and encouragement in grappling with debt? The widow could only bear witness to the miraculous powers of God when she realized she needed help, heard and obeyed instruction, and stepped out on faith.

4

Giving

"...and to remember the words of the Lord Jesus, how He said, It is more blessed to give than to receive." (Acts 20:35 KJV)

If God took a history test and it was worth 100 points, how many points do you think He would score? What if you gave God a math test, how well do you think He would do? Do you think He would get a perfect score? Well, what if you put bonus points on the test? Do you think He would get all of the bonus points correct? How many of us think that God would have trouble with those tests? We are confident that God can pass any test that we can create. Well, almost any test. It is interesting that when God asks us to test Him through our giving, we lose confidence in Him. In Malachi 3:10, God asked us to:

"Bring the whole tithe into the storehouse, that there may be food in my house. Test me in this," says the LORD Almighty, "and see if I will not throw open the floodgates of heaven and pour out so much blessing that you will not have room enough for it."(Malachi 3:10 NIV).

When we bring our tithes to the storehouse, we are being obedient to God. God is also letting us know that we are giving Him an opportunity to take a test. He says that we can test Him and see how well He performs. He tells us that He will pour out an abundance of blessings into our lives. Basically God is saying that if you give Him a test, He will score well, but you get the benefit of His perfect score. I can testify to God's ability to pass this test. Ever since my wife and I have brought our tithes to the storehouse, God has blessed us. We are able to do so much more with the 90% then we ever did with the full 100%.

God's financial plan for our lives places an emphasis on giving. Not only does God lay out what He wants us to give, He also instructs us on the proper attitude for giving. He then shares with us some promises for those that obey Him in their giving. That is why a strong financial house will have giving as one of its bricks.

Through inspiration of God, Paul writes:

"I have shewed you all things, how that so labouring ye ought to support the weak, and to remember the words of the Lord Jesus, how He said, 'It is more blessed to give than to receive'" (Acts 20:35 KJV)

Paul is addressing the elders of a church in Ephesus. He is encouraging them to remember that Jesus Christ said that it is more blessed to give than receive. How can we be more blessed when we give, than receive? Well, when we take the position of a giver, we are lining ourselves up to be poured into. We will be poured into because God knows that what He pours out to you will be shared with others.

God's Word has promises for those that give generously, and you can rest on them. However, we must understand that God's word is clear on the attitude that must exist in us as we give. In I Corinthians 13:3, we are taught:

"And though I bestow all my goods to feed the poor, and though I give my body to be burned, and have not charity, it profiteth me nothing." (1 Corinthians 13:3 KJV)

We can invest in others by feeding the poor, or some other act of charity, but not have love in our heart. God's Word says that without love, we will not yield a profit. Profit is money we are allowed to keep that is above what we invested. God's money management tells us that giving is like investing. When we have the right attitude, we can receive a profit from it. That does not mean we will always receive a monetary profit. Our profit could come by keeping us from sickness. It could also come by keeping our loved ones safe. In order to receive the profit from our gifts, we must give with the proper attitude of love. That is what God did when He gave his Son. John 3:16 begins with the announcement that *"For God so loved the world, that He gave..."* God loves us so much. His love came before His gift.

Now that we have settled the matter on the proper attitude for giving, we must now allow God's Word to instruct us on how much to give. The first recorded instance of giving to a representative of God was in Genesis 14:20. The scripture states that

"And blessed be God Most High, who delivered your enemies into your hand." Then Abram gave him a tenth of everything." (Genesis 14:20 NIV)

The beginning of Genesis 14 talks about a number of kings taking over Sodom and Gomorrah and taking Lot captive. Abram, with God's help, rescues Lot and brings him back, along with the "spoils" from the fighting. On his way back, he encounters King Melchizedek. The Bible says that King Melchizedek was the priest of the most High God.

Scholars have suggested that this King could be an Old Testament appearance of the Son of God. Regardless of how he is viewed, this King is still considered a holy figure. Abram honors this "priest of the most High" by giving him a tenth of everything. This is an Old Testament example of honoring God with a tenth of everything.

Some ask whether the tithe is a tenth of your gross pay or a tenth of your net pay. The Bible is clear that we are to give of our first fruits. I personally believe that the conversation about gross or net is sometimes motivated by a desire to figure out how much can be kept. At that point, is that cheerful, sacrificial giving? Abram's model in God's word tells us that he gave a tenth of everything. We are also taught to give of our first fruits. I was having lunch with an authority on Biblical financial principles, and he shared something that stuck with me. The question he raised is, would you rather be blessed on the gross or the net?

I think it is important to understand that your salvation is not tied to your giving. As we talk about giving, we are talking about obedience to God. By being obedient to God, we are putting ourselves in position to receive His promised blessings. We must remember that our Savior came that we may have life and have it more abundantly. We must hear and obey the instructions that He gives us concerning the proper attitude towards giving so that we may partake in that abundant life that He promises.

Now that we have identified the proper attitude concerning giving and the amount, we can now rejoice because of the promise God has given to us for our obedience to His giving principles. This is a blessing that goes unclaimed in the lives of many Christians. God is the ultimate investor. When individuals invest in the stock market, they invest in stocks that they believe will increase in value. They will invest some of their money in the hopes that they will get that money back, as well as an increase. If they put $8,000 in, they hope to maybe double their investment to $16,000.

Proverbs 11:24-25 gives us a wonderful illustration of God's ability to invest in places where He knows He will get the greatest return. The Bible says that

"One man gives freely, yet gains even more; another withholds unduly, but comes to poverty. A generous man will prosper; he who refreshes others will himself be refreshed." (Proverbs 11:24-25 NIV)

As the man gives freely, he gains even more. The generous man refreshes others and because of this, he himself will be refreshed. When our obedience to God manifests itself through our giving, we are taught that God will refresh the person who is refreshing others. As we give freely of our tithes and offerings, God will prosper us through refreshing us as we refresh others.

It is very important to keep in mind that the benefits of giving are not provided as motivators for us to give. They are used by God to reward our obedience and to show others that He blesses those who have the right attitude toward giving.

5

Saving and Investing

"The plans of the diligent lead to profit as surely as haste leads to poverty."
(Proverbs 21:5 NIV)

Another biblical truth that goes into building a strong financial house deals with saving money. We all have a part of our house that has gotten cluttered over the years. Year after year, this space in our house has accumulated stuff. For some, it could be the garage. For others, it could be the attic. For me, it is the storage closet in our basement. When you think about it, these areas of the house got that way based on years and years of accumulating stuff. As we think about those cluttered spaces, we often wonder how we accumulated so much. It was a long, slow process of putting things in that spot, and forgetting about them. One day, we go to that spot to put more in, and we find that the spot is overflowing with all the things we put in there. What if we applied that same process in our savings? God's Word encourages us to save. That is why a strong financial house must be built on the biblical principles of savings.

We are good at accumulating stuff but not necessarily good at accumulating money. According to a recent study done by the US Bureau of Economic Analysis, the percentage of our income that we save has declined at an alarming rate. In the second quarter of 2006, our personal savings rate was at an alarming –1.5%[1]. Yes, you are reading that right. We actually managed to save a negative percent of our income. Well, what does that mean? If we earned $100.00 and saved nothing, we would have a personal savings rate of 0%. A 0% savings rate is alarming by itself. That means we are spending all of our money and not saving. In Proverbs 21:20, we are taught that:

"In the house of the wise are stores of choice food and oil, but a foolish man devours all he has."(Proverbs 21:20 NIV)

A 0% savings rate means that we are devouring all that we have without storing up anything. If 0% is bad, a negative personal savings rate is cause for more alarm. Somehow, we managed to spend more money than we actually earn. We earned $100.00 but spent $113.00. How do we do that? You guessed it—credit cards. A negative personal savings rate puts our financial house in an insecure situation. Without proper savings, our financial house would be vulnerable to all types of "Hurricane Katrina" moments. "Katrina" reminds us all of the importance of having adequate savings to weather storms. I listened to finance related talk radio shows in the aftermath of "Katrina." People who were affected by Katrina would call in to share their stories. Some of them would rejoice over the fact that they had money saved up to weather the storm. They had money to secure adequate housing, secure food, purchase additional clothing, and take care of themselves for a few months. Their savings helped them to weather the storm a little bit more easily.

Through biblical principles in God's Word, we are taught His will for our financial lives as it relates to saving and investing. Let's unpack some of these scriptures and then identify some practical strategies that have helped my family save money. In Genesis 41, we find out that the Pharaoh had two dreams that he could not understand. One of the dreams dealt with seven sickly cows eating up seven healthy cows. The Pharaoh's other dream dealt with seven thin grains eating up seven healthy grains. He could not understand his dream so he summoned some of his magicians and wise men to help him interpret the dream. They were not able to interpret the dream. Notice here that even though the Pharaoh sought advice, he went to the wrong people for advice. We must remember to seek the counsel of prayer, the scriptures, as well as counsel from godly people.

When the magicians and wise men failed to interpret the dreams, the Pharaoh's cupbearer remembered Joseph and his ability to interpret dreams. The Pharaoh then summoned Joseph to come from the prison. Joseph came and helped the Pharaoh understand the dreams. God was letting the Pharaoh know that Egypt was about to have seven years of abundance and then seven years of famine. I think it is awesome that God let Pharaoh know that famine was coming. While God can, He does not choose to reveal the exact times of our financially abundant season or the exact time of our famine seasons. For this reason, we must always be ready when our season of famine comes upon us. In Genesis 41:34-36, the scripture says:

"Let Pharaoh appoint commissioners over the land to take a fifth of the harvest of Egypt during the seven years of abundance. They should collect all the food of these good years that are coming and store up the grain under the authority of Pharaoh, to be kept in the cities for food. This food should be held in reserve for the country, to be used during the seven years of famine that will come upon Egypt, so that the country may not be ruined by the famine." (Genesis 41:34-36 NIV)

We are instructed to take a fifth of the harvest during our seven years of abundance. How can we apply this to our financial lives today? We are encouraged to save a portion of our resources during good times. We must develop the habit of saving. The fifth of our resources must be held in reserve to be used during our season of famine. In my work as a tax and money advisor, I tell my clients to establish an emergency fund of $1,000.00 at first. We will discuss other specific steps as we move through our discussion on savings.

God instructs us on the manner in which we should save. In Proverbs 21:5, we are taught that *"The plans of the diligent lead to profit as surely as haste leads to poverty." (Proverbs 21:5 NIV)* We have to have a plan for saving money, and we must be diligent in our plan. Diligent means *"constant in effort or exertion to accomplish what is undertaken"*[2] We must develop a plan to save and then consistently put forth effort to accomplish the plan. God's Word lets us know that diligent planning leads to profit. If we choose to go the quick route through lottery tickets, or gambling, or get-rich-quick schemes, we are warned that those actions lead to poverty. Do you have a plan that you consistently put forth effort to accomplish? If you don't, I would like to offer some suggestions. These suggestions have proven to be effective time and time again in the lives of those that choose to follow them. I hope you choose to use them.

Step 1: Determine your net worth

In Proverbs 27:23-24, we are taught to

"Be sure you know the condition of your flocks, give careful attention to your herds; for riches do not endure forever and a crown is not secure for all generations." (Proverbs 27:23-24 NIV)

In biblical times, your flocks determined your financial status. They represented your assets. God encourages us to know how our assets are doing and to pay attention to them. How do we do this? We must calculate our Net Worth. Net Worth is simply the dollar amount after we subtract all of our debt from the value of all of our assets. You can value your assets by simply adding up the value of your house, your car, your bank account, stocks, etc. For example, you can find the value of your home by finding out what a house on your street that was similar to yours recently sold for. You can identify the value of your car using sites such as Kelly Blue Book. Once you have figured out the value of what you OWN, you must now figure out how much you OWE. You can use the same list that you created when you were dealing with the chapter on debt. What you owe is your mortgage, car note, credit card debt, and any other debt that you may have. Those who dwell in a strong financial house have a high net worth because its possessions are a much greater value than what they owe. Go to www. FredWallerMinistries.com, and you will find financial tools that you can use to calculate your Net Worth. Do not be discouraged if your net worth is not where you want it to be. Most people start off with a negative Net Worth. If you are not happy, let that be your motivation to increase your net worth through reducing your debt.

Step 2: Establish an Emergency Fund

I was listening to a radio show and heard a wonderful ad. The ad started off with a phone ringing. When the actor answered the phone, he hears the operator say to him,

"This is your future calling and I need you to sit down. I just wanted to give you a call to let you know that in two months your washing machine will break, and in three months, your car will need major engine work, and then in 5 months you will need some repairs done to your roof!"

The response from the actor was,

"Thanks so much. I'm glad you called. Now, I can start saving for those emergencies. If you had not called, I would not have been prepared for those setbacks."

We all wish that we could get warned about upcoming financial emergencies. Unfortunately, it does not work like that. However, we have lived long enough to know that financial emergencies do happen. For some reason, they always seem to happen when we least expect them. Developing an emergency fund needs to be a top priority. This is even more important then eliminating debt. I recommend that people start with a goal of saving $1,000 in a bank account. If you are paying extra on your credit card, you should stop until you have your emergency fund up to $1,000. If you are investing in your 401K, but don't have an emergency fund, you should temporarily suspend your 401K investing. Notice I said temporarily. Some might argue that stopping your 401K is bad financial advice considering the free company match. However, when emergencies happen and there are no savings, you would go straight to the 401K for a loan. Not only do you open yourself up to potential tax consequences, but you also begin a dangerous trend of seeing your 401K as an emergency fund. A 401K is strictly for long term retirement planning. So, make sure you get an emergency fund.

Step 3: Invest in company investment plans

After you have your net worth calculated, your emergency fund set aside, and you're following an aggressive plan for eliminating debt, you should then invest in your company investment plans. Most employers now have 401K's and/or 403B's. The 401K typically is provided by companies in the private sector such as banking, or other corporate jobs. The 403B is similar to the 401K and is typically provided by public employers like school districts, hospitals, etc. I strongly encourage participating in your employer's retirement plan. Now let me reiterate an important point by saying that you don't want to do any investing until you are totally free of debt except for the house. By totally paying off debt, you are freeing up the money that you were previously using to pay off debt, and now are able to use that to contribute fully to your employer retirement plans. As Lynette and I were aggressively paying off our debt, we were spending $600 per month to pay off debt. Once that debt was paid, we were able to allocate that money to other options that both fully funded our budget and allowed us to save and invest more. Once you are done paying off all your debts, and also have settled the matter within yourself that you will not go back to owing anybody any money, you can then take the former debt payments and invest in your company's investment plans. Now I should also say that your company's' investment plans often have options that may be confusing to you. That is when you remember the foundation brick that tells you to seek out and listen to wise counsel. Contact a financial advisor you can trust to give you sound advice. If you are in the Central Pennsylvania area, I am available for money coaching.

Step 4: Diversify

I know that you have heard the cliché *"Don't put all your eggs in one basket."* Given the recent corporate financial scandals that caused thousands of their employees to lose some, if not all, of their retirement money, this cliché is incredibly necessary to apply. As you begin to explore investments, you must be mindful to diversify. Because of these types of scandals, it is very risky not to diversify. A good mutual fund does well to diversify your savings.

6

Proper Estate Planning

"A good man leaveth an inheritance to his children's children: and the wealth of the sinner is laid up for the just." (Proverbs 13:22 KJV)

A strong financial house will have a foundation built on the Word of God. It will also have four walls that are reinforced with biblical principles. The final part of a strong financial house is the roof. Without a strong roof, a storm can come by and knock the roof off and the walls would fall and the foundation could be damaged. This final component of our financial house deals with making sure we properly handle the needs that arise when we die. We are talking about proper estate planning. I came across a very powerful saying that helps to bring home the importance of proper estate planning. I know that while death is probably the most uncomfortable thing to talk about, we must remember that:

"The time of our death is unknown. The way of our death is unpredictable. The FACT of our death is inescapable." (author unknown)

The Word of God helps us to understand the importance of proper estate planning as well. A very popular passage that needs to be highlighted is the scripture in Proverbs 13:22. The scripture says that:

"A good man leaveth an inheritance to his children's children: and the wealth of the sinner is laid up for the just."

What is powerful about this text is that we are taught that the Word of God considers a man who leaves an inheritance to his children's children to be a good man. We can provide for our family when we are alive; however, the final determining factor for our reputation is whether we put our family in a good or bad situation when we pass away. Remember the man of God who left his widow and two sons with debt. We notice in II Kings 4:1-7 that the husband who died served God and probably was considered to be a good man during his life. Unfortunately, he did not leave an inheritance for his children and was noted in scripture for his failure to provide, not for his work while he was living.

The scripture goes on to talk about the wealth of a non-believer being stored for the believer. God ultimately will provide for His people just like He did for the widow in II Kings 4:1-7. However, we should take steps to do our part in providing for our family. We must have adequate life insurance.

There are so many different formulas that are used to decide how much insurance we should have. Some would say ten times our present yearly income. Some would argue eight times our present salary. In my opinion, from a biblical point of view, we only need enough life insurance to make sure that all of our debts and obligations are taken care of. Life insurance should not be used as a way of making our families rich. If that is God's will for our families, He will make it happen. We need to calculate what our financial obligations would be if we passed away and make sure we have enough life insurance to cover those obligations. Some of our obligations upon our death are making sure there is money for our children's education. We must also provide for the expenses of the funeral. We must also make sure that our spouses are not put in a difficult situation trying to replace your income. Life insurance should replace your income for at least 10 years or so.

The "how to" is important, but, not as important as the "how come." We must realize that the Word of God considers us to be good men when we leave inheritances to our children's children. Now single mothers are included in this definition of good men. It is extremely important for single mothers to make sure life insurance is in place. Before the week is out, make sure you go get the appropriate amount of life insurance. Deal with it once, and, for the most part, you'll never have to worry about it again.

After we secure insurance against our premature death, we must then establish our last will and testament. The Bible also gives us clear instruction when we see the prophet Isaiah being obedient to God, letting Hezekiah know in 2 Kings 20:1:

"...This is what the Lord says: Put your house in order, because you are going to die, you will not recover." (II Kings 20:1 NIV)

Now, we learn later in the scripture that Hezekiah's prayer ultimately led God to heal him. Even though God decided to remove him from the clutches of death, he still was charged to *"Put [his] house in order"* We get our house in order through adequate insurance and also making sure we have a will. Our will serves the purpose of communicating our final instructions for the property that we have accumulated.

The Word of God also gives us clear instructions on what we must be mindful of in our will. For those of us who have children, we must make sure that our children don't get a large inheritance until they are capable of dealing with it sensibly. If that does not happen, there is a great risk that the inheritance will be squandered on electronic gadgets, cars, and/or clothes. The Bible lets us know that we must establish trusted guardians for our children so that they don't squander their inheritance blown. The Bible records in Galatians 4:1-2 that

"What I am saying is that as long as the heir is a child, he is no different from a slave, although he owns the whole estate. He is subject to guardians and trustees until the time set by his father." (Galatians 4:1-2 NIV)

This scripture lets us know that the estate in the hands of a child is not desirable at all. The child must be

"subject to guardians and trustees until the time set by his father."

The guardians and trustees are established in the will by the father. We must establish the proper time in which the child is capable of making good decisions concerning the money left in an inheritance.

I should also take this time to highlight some other important decisions that need to be made so that the roof will never blow off your strong financial house. The first thing is to remember to invest in disability insurance. Some employers provide short and long-term disability. If your employer does not have it, you should purchase it on your own. In my career as a tax and money "coach", I have constantly encouraged all of my self-employed clients to invest in some type of disability insurance. My clients would sometimes argue that they could not afford to pay for disability insurance while they are growing their business. I would tell them that they could not afford to not pay for disability insurance. Get disability insurance to protect your income should you have a prolonged illness or disability and cannot work.

It is important to remember that proper estate planning is vital to a strong financial house. Being a good man or woman is ultimately measured upon your death. Did you die and leave an inheritance or did you die and leave debt? With proper estate planning, we will leave the inheritance and earn a good name. We must also make sure we have a will that communicates our wishes as it relates to the transferring of our wealth to our surviving family members.

7

I Realize "How Come",
Now What?

The six bricks that make up a strong financial house are crucial to insure liberation from financial bondage.

The first brick reveals strong biblical truths that can mold our thinking about money. This is the foundational brick of the Word of God which calls for us to listen and be obedient to all of His teachings. We must give up ownership and stop thinking that it is our stuff. We must properly manage the resources that God has blessed us with. We must also seek wise counsel.

The second brick reveals the biblical principle of having a good name. We need to know what our credit score has to say about us. We should check our credit reports for any false information. If we find any false information, we should dispute it through the proper procedures. We also need to pay our bills on time. The "divide and conquer" method to pay bills can allow you to consistently pay your bills on time and increase your credit score in the process.

The third brick lets us know that the borrower is servant to the lender. We must begin a debt reduction plan. We must diligently work that debt reduction plan. Our diligence will be honored with success. That success will motivate us to continue until we are totally out of debt.

The fourth brick reveals the requirements of giving. Our giving is our faith test. There are many scriptures that promise God's supernatural favor when we walk by faith and not by sight. Look at Abraham's faith test as it relates to giving. In the 22nd chapter of Genesis, we are shown Abraham's walk of faith. He was asked to sacrifice Isaac as an offering back to God. That is a faith walk. I mean an incredible faith walk. If you examine that passage of scripture, you would realize that Abraham had to walk at least three days to sacrifice his son. He had plenty of time to let his faith fail him and to turn around. He did not and after God saw his faith, He was pleased and then provided for Abraham. The three Hebrew boys stepped out on faith as they faced the fiery furnace. When their faith was tested, they passed, and God showed up to deliver them from the fiery furnace. I can't convince you to give. If I talk you into it, your life situation will talk you out of it. All I can say is that I can testify that since my wife and I have tithed 10% of our gross pay, we have been tremendously blessed.

The fifth brick reveals the biblical principles that teach us about saving and investing. Don't forget that the Word of God challenges us to store up during good times to help us get through the bad times. As much as we would love this to happen, we are not going to be given a two month warning before a financial crisis. Because of that, we need to develop a plan for saving and diligently follow the plan. When all debt is paid off, and you have a fully funded emergency fund, begin the "steady plodding" into an appropriate investment.

The final brick reveals the biblical principle that guides us in proper estate planning. I don't want to be the bearer of bad news, but we all are going to breathe our last breath someday. I don't mean to be morbid, but we must not ignore the fact that God tells us in Hebrews 9:27 that we are destined to die once. Knowing that, God urges us to put our house in order with the appropriate life insurance and a proper will.

As I conclude, I want you to remember that this book is primarily a "how come" book. I also want you to use this as a resource book to be referred back to. When you put it on the coffee table, make sure it is the one on top. There are plenty of books that talk about the "how to" of money management. I believe that the "how come" is the crucial first step. By getting you to understand "how come," I hope I have created a hunger for the "how to." It has been my prayer throughout its writing that this book be a tool of God to begin the transformation of your mind concerning your finances. This transformation process is not instantaneous. It is an ongoing process. This is just the beginning on your road to freedom from financial bondage. Along the way, you WILL need to make pit stops and "fill up" your gas tank. The "fill-ups" are for the next part of your journey towards financial freedom. Here are some opportunities to "fill up."

My website offers more information about what the Word of God has to say about managing money. There are resources that are provided for your continued education. My website is:

www.FredWallerMinistries.com

I do a monthly radio program that I produce from home and send out to subscribers. In this monthly broadcast, you can hear me discuss a variety of money management topics from a biblical point of view. The broadcast is free and easy to subscribe to. My website will have the instructions on how to automatically receive the broadcast every month totally free.

Automobile University is also a great place to enroll. What do I mean by Automobile University? Automobile University is basically just using the tape or CD player in your car to listen to books on tape that talk about different aspects of money management. Instead of just using your car stereo to blast the latest hot song, use it to teach you about money. My website has some recommended book titles on tape that you can purchase.

I would also recommend investing in subscriptions to financial magazines. These magazines provide timely money management strategies on a monthly basis which helps you to gas up at least once a month. I have some recommended titles at my website.

I would also recommend that you find an accountability partner whom you will allow to hold you accountable for this new walk concerning proper money management. I am the accountability partner for my tax and investment clients in Pennsylvania. Feel free to contact me at www.FredWallerMinistries.com to allow me to work with you to achieve your financial goals.

Thank you for your time, and I pray for financial breakthroughs in your life. Just make sure your financial house is built with God's biblical truths. By doing this, the truth shall set you financially free.

APPENDIX

List of your debts

Who do you owe?	Phone Number	Total owed as of _____ (date)	Interest Rate

Notes

Introduction

1. United States. Federal Reserve Statistical Release. <u>Consumer Debt.</u> 10 July. 2006. 1 Aug.2006. <u>http://www.federalreserve.gov/releases/g19/current/</u>

Chapter 1

1. Psalms 50:10

2. Haggai 2:8

3. I Kings 3:12

4. "Entry for 'Hearken'". "King James Dictionary". <http://www.studylight.org/dic/kjd/view.cgi?number=T2818>.

Chapter 2

1. Mark 3:25

Chapter 3

1. "Entry for 'Servant'". "King James Dictionary". <http://www.studylight.org/dic/kjd/view.cgi?number=T5035>.

2. Matthew 6:24

3. Downing, Eve. "The psychology of spending: The urge to splurge."*Spectrvm:Massachusetts Institute of Technology.* Winter 1999. 3 Aug. 2006. <http://web.mit.edu/giving/spectrum/winter99/spending.html>

4. **Source:** "Americans are 'spending' themselves into unhappiness," *Baylor Business Review*, Spring2000.

Chapter 5

1. "Personal Savings Rate." US Bureau of Economic Analysis. 28 July 2006. <http://www.bea.gov/briefrm/savings.htm>

2. "Entry for 'Diligent'". "King James Dictionary". <http://www.studylight.org/dic/kjd/view.cgi?number=T1638>.

Meet Fred Waller

Entrepreneur, Teacher, Speaker, Author

"My purpose in life is to share God's word to help others break free from financial bondage."

—Fred Waller

"What fascinates me is his broad and effective use of Scripture to present and substantiate his positions. One gets the sense readily that this is not Fred, himself, speaking; rather it is the Holy Spirit revealing truth to him and his willingness to pass it on to us."

—Pastor Louis A. Butcher, Jr.
Bright Side Baptist Church

Fred Waller has a Bachelor's degree in Mathematics Education. He is a Deacon and Education Ministry Chair at Bright Side Baptist Church in Pennsylvania. He owns and operates Waller Tax and Money Advisors, a tax and money-consulting firm where he helps hundreds of people with both their tax and money management needs. He is a Certified Budget Coach through Crown Financial Ministries. He has been living and teaching biblical principles of money management for many years in Pennsylvania.

Using Biblical principles, thought-provoking analogies, and a keen sense of humor, Fred remains in constant demand as a speaker and workshop facilitator at conferences, churches, retreats, revivals, and seminars.

His experience has made him uniquely qualified to teach on a variety of topics:

<u>Keynote and Workshop Topics:</u>

Six Bricks of a Strong Financial House
Deliverance from Debt
Why Seek Financial Counsel?

For more information, call 717-394-5793 or go to
www.FredWallerMinistries.com

978-0-595-40696-8
0-595-40696-3

Printed in the United States
64057LVS00002B/127-324